SIMPLY F

TO BE READ AN

BOB LOCK

Acknowledgments

Searching - First published by First Time Magazine
A Daughter's Lost Shoe - First published by Exile

Published in 2000 by Bob Lock
1 Gleneagles Court, Mafeking Road, Chatham, Kent
ISBN 0-9539693-0-4

Illustrations and creative concept by Bill Daniels
Design, layout and typesetting by Gail Everett
Printed and bound by Reader and Phillips, Gillingham, Kent

PREFACE

A poem is something special - deserving of its own presence, given life from the inanimate. Born of its own character - nurtured to an entity, allowed space, a full introduction as does an individual. After all, each poem is individually moulded to portray thoughts and situations, regardless of its simplicity or depth.

The poem has no dependence on life's sustenance but once born is eternal. Reliant not on the hand of fate but on the hand that turns each page, posterity its beneficiary.

Each poem of this miscellany is introduced in its own right - portraying the message or innuendo but never losing sight of the prime purpose, TO BE READ AND ENJOYED.

CONTENTS

OPENING DOORS

Doors open, doors close
No particular phenomenon.
Some say 'One opens - one closes'.
Clichés accepted, no major problem.
Except when entering doors from
Which others only emerge or,
Emerging from those which
Others only enter. Or maybe
Trapped in those revolving,
Seeking life on both sides.
Doors can lead everywhere
Sometimes nowhere, some half open
Some half closed, entry or departure
Dependent on fortune or fate.
Some leave doors open and
Others bolt them firmly shut
But worry most, when doors
That you knock - are never opened.

SEARCHING

in the mind and behind the eyes of the writer

Emphasis lies predominantly in the desire of all forms of life to seek answers, search, and question. The opening stanza recognises Night as an inanimate force, contriving to create a situation to monitor the reactions of manipulated objects. The requiem 'Chant to Death', being the soul searching of these.

Flap winged bats in "silent flight' refers to the usual noisy flapping sound – now suppressed to use their (Radar) inbuilt control to furtively seek, using the shafts of light for added direction. (This light provided by moon beams) who in their turn are searching, although being thwarted by darkness and clouds. The Yew Tree traditionally very old and long living (hence ancient) used in the second line, in its structural make up a complete disfiguration, to fool the observers but using its roots as antennae to discover what is happening in the Hallowed (Church Yard) Ground. The Oak Tree is now converted to a coffin containing body and 'Souls' who are perhaps searching for new meaning and objectives, only to return to the musty earth wherein lies their Destiny.

SEARCHING

Night nurtures dark cloaked effigies
In sombre stance, mid ancient trees.
Viewing their wizened warps
With deep held breath,
Awaiting a requiem chant to death.

Flap winged bats in silent flight
Radar in on shafts of light,
As moonbeams dart from darkened clouds
In stern defiance of night-time's shroud.

The yew that so long has stood,
A cynical interweave of wood.
With roots sunk deep in hallowed ground
Seeking answers - yet unfound.

Buried lies the related oak
Encasing souls, perhaps in flight
Searching mysteries of the night.
Musty mould, the tombs surround
Awaits their return and answer found.

JOURNEYS TOO LATE

The sea carries,
All but those who
In dreams journey.
Or skies lift those who
Travel on imagination's wing.
Leaving only floating clouds
And fleeting shadows
On which to reflect.
The moon dusts
Far off shores,
Unvisited beaches
Other feet now tread.
Blurring the vision with sand
That trickles, like a timer
In the mind's eye.
Pebbled shores
Crave attendance
In stony silence.
Awaiting once heavy feet,
That now so lightly tread
An impromptu stairway.
Its destination, of fate's
Design and choosing
As time runs out.

THE FISHERMAN

Hair, salt bleached tangled grey
Rugged tan of burnished gold.
Channels all knowledge through
Age wise eyes, piercing blue.

Roughened hands, like bark of tree
Portrays the hook's deep bite, and
Four fingered proof of wayward knife.
His desire, not on land to rest
Finds 'terra-firma' second best.

Salty brine, scourging lungs
Wreaks havoc for landlubber sons,
For whom the sea cares far less
As lost bodies - and kin's distress.

Gulls screech shrill demands,
Feel their need more great than man's
As roars the sea's mighty swell
In defiance of alien vessels' cull.

And on seas born free
No shroud for humanity,
Now his task, set full sail
In the ocean fury's hell.

UNFORGIVING

Forbidden fruit, once sweet turns sour
When in retrospect devoured.
Shrouded in collusion's cloak
Close knit by deception's hand,
Woven then each stitch and thread
Born of folly's wayward tread.

Now the tender shell's first flaw
As from wall the egg does fall.
Conscience thus laid bare
Fragmented by wrath's shatter,
In its grounded spew there lies
The yolk of forgiveness in demise.

Released emotions coiling
The hand of fate embroiling,
Our flighty hare now jugged.
Aborted, vestige of any hope
As love, the victim of all lies
Now in retribution - dies.

PLEA TO A 'TWISTER'

Oh, mighty wind, you blow so loud
To disturb the very shroud
Of humanity.
Seek not to invade our living dreams
Or tear apart the very seams.
Such wrath and power you dispose!
Pray wreak not vengeance with each gust
Nor taunt us with your wanderlust.

Of your mighty spiral in the sky
In fear we mortals go. When shown the strength
Of your hand
Pray, hold us less close.
We are but flesh and blood in humility,
In awe of your fearsome symmetry.
To watch you move earth and sea,
Tread soft, lest too late we flee.

As dusk shields our sight,
Pass us by, fix us not with
Your inner eye,
Lest we perish in your wake,
Your anger will fade to oblivion
When that titanic strength has gone.
Look back in mercy as you move away
That all may see another day.

A DAUGHTER'S LOST SHOE

Hearts then young, happy hours spent
In the Garden of England - Kent.
Nurtured thoughts of those days
As in warmth of summer lays
Fordwich - Wickhambreaux.

A mighty oak, king of trees
Cooling the brow with summer leaves
The wooden bridge, where lost her shoe
In the river that saunters through
Fordwich - Wickhambreaux.

Soulful the look of self-reproach
That on heartstrings did encroach.
On her face a trace of tear
To pierce the heart like a spear
Fordwich - Wickhambreaux.

Although time now rings its toll
Remains the memory within my soul,
Fordwich - Wickhambreaux.

A SONG OF THE MEDWAY

Two score and more years since
First I stood 'twixt bridge and bank
Of the Medway
Neither Man of Kent nor Kentish Man.
But blissfully at peace
With each crossing of that bridge,
Like entering a home land gifted by fate.
From Cockney birth, then southern climes,
No better times than since
My first journey across Rochester Bridge.
No grand or majestic structure but,
Entry still to contentment and happiness.
How many have made that journey?
On carriage, horse or foot
To be greeted by nearby hostelries,
Their welcome in the river's reflections.
Many a night have stars
Brightened their path, to reach
Their Journey's End - or travel on.
History and spectacle abound to make
Rochester one of England's special cities.
Dickensian memorabilia merging,
With ancient structural beauty.
So many changes seen since those days
When Richard Watts, gave the down on luck
A resting place for the night and
Assistance to continue their journey,
Many stayed.
The castle could tell of 'Far Off' days
Of serf and slave.

Battles with sword and arrow.
If only it could speak,
It would talk for many a week.
Now where factories have come, and gone.
Comfortable, Elegant Houses and Apartments
Smile cynically, at industry's loss.
What price to us - what cost?
I muse - "only two score years and more"
Not long, but long enough to sing
"A song of the Medway".
This song I sing has no sound.
No melody to calm or soothe
No instruments or interlude.
Music and Lyrics to this theme
Like its rhythm, just a dream.
Its chorus and notes our future hopes,
Our future hopes and many a thing
That goes to make - a glad heart, sing.
In this silent refrain,
No use for lock, bolts or chain.
A song, whose score,
Is seen only through window
And open door.

Now to sit and ponder
What lies ahead?
As that silent river wends its way
And dusk ends another day.
Each moment its swirling water
Like life - fades away.

THE GARDEN OF ENGLAND

When my "get up and go"
Got up and went,
That was the day I
Moved into Kent.
Hop fields in plenty
Orchards and trees
A lightly slung hammock
That swayed in the breeze.
Farmyards and chickens
Ducks by the score
Peace and tranquillity
Here at the door,
Windmills and oasts
Their working days spent.
Why don't you come join
Me? – Down here in Kent.

FROM ON A HILL
(MY VILLAGE BY NIGHT)

As here we stand – set on high
It seems almost, mid earth and sky
Such a view must surely prise
A trace of tear from each one's eyes.
Below, the plots and dwellings stand
Metred out by metric hand –
Staking the lineage of our land.
And each brick within each wall
Or garden fence standing tall,
Holding all in tight cocoon
On display, by light of moon.
Built from metal, brick and breeze
Captured by the ribboned frieze
Of street lamps piercing, dark of night
Forming this vision of delight.
Nocturne's cloak, now close drawn
In silent laze till break of dawn.
Herein lie the hopes and dreams
Of faceless ones, to us it seems.
In secluded comfort of each room,
Lost from view and light of moon
Who shines more bright, to foretell
The nightly ritual of this spell.
Woven now as each we stand
Witness to, by God's own hand
Whose safe grasp feels more tight
Held in comfort of the night.

GAMBLERS UNANIMOUS

Just another racing day,
So-called 'pundits' lead the way.
Elation as the tipsters feed
Our fantasies and inner needs.
Their predictions on a thousand lips
And myriad of betting slips.
Time to lay that redeeming stake
Each risk keeping our hopes awake.
'Chance the arm' - pay the price!

'Find the Lady', 'Spot the Ball',
Name the forecast, did yours fall?
"Second fence, can't understand -
33's worth a grand
If it had won!"
Catastrophe! 'St Louis Blues',
Have you heard the latest news?
Racing on Sundays - that's all right!
But what about Sunday night?
Watch the telly?
Feed the cat?
Activate the 'Old Dead Rat'?
I tell you friend, "Let's have no mirth"
No gambling? Must be hell on earth!

UP SHIT'S CREEK

Finding myself marooned
In a particularly smelly backwater.
I placed an advert in the
Local 'Rag' - seeking purchase of
A "Second hand" Paddle.
No longer enjoying affluence.

WHEN THE COUNTING STARTS

Gone those years
Sixty and eight.
What, tomorrow
Shall await?
Life, now unkind
My frailties you find.

A TOUCHING SITUATION

She had a passion for
Silk Gloves,
Needing to feel at home
With herself.

MARRIED TO A MOVIE STAR

We were in bed
I gave her
A mirror, that she
Might have her pleasure
Whilst I had mine.

EMOTIONAL INVOLVEMENT

I will enjoy
The match to-day
I shall cry
- Whoever loses.

GRASPING THE SITUATION

I put my hand around it.
Why, I just can't
Put my finger on it.

CUPBOARD LOVE

Have I told you about my
Amorous cutlery and tableware?
It transpires much woo(ing)
To(ing) and Fro(ing) has been
Going on behind my back.
Plates taking a shine to dishes
Only to finish all washed up.
Knives and spoons in close
Embrace, finding their relationship
Severely shaken by forked tongues.
Drinking vessels cupping hands
Around each other, finding
Their grasp hard to handle.
Dinner plates enjoying snug loving
Contact finishing in tears.
Saucers their saucy antics
Dampened – Now in deep water.
Killing nursery rhyme stone dead,
The dish and the spoon
Have recently parted company,
Deciding to go their separate ways.
Now, they have all run away
With the dishwasher
Who, it would appear
IS ANYBODY'S!

A COMPLETE SERVICE, UNDERTAKEN

The wife of John - a packaging boffin
Approached us to supply a light-weight coffin.
But before the time of his demise
Was unaware of the impending surprise.
Apparently John, of whom it was said
"Spent his last earthly moments in bed"
Was known to have died in excitements prime
Hence the reason for his 'incline',
Which made it hard for Terrence and Syd
Whose job it was to close the lid.
Syd then phoned us with a stutter and stammer,
So we sent in our team, with nails and a hammer
To close the lid and fulfil our promise
Of service 'extended' to each John
- And Thomas!

A RAPIST IN PICCADILLY CIRCUS

All it needs is a number 9 bus
To satisfy his journey of lust,
Or a short walk from Charing Cross
After all, he is the boss –
Of licentiousness!
No hearts burst in abject despair;
No-one knows of his presence there.
Where 'Eros' stands and tourists abound
Midst the comfort of shops and underground.
As each maiden passes by,
He looses the devil from wanton eye.
To visit his kingdom of lustful dream
Where the pink pointer reigns supreme.

May his visit be but brief
His presence worse than the pigeon's relief
Their release but lime and grit
His a mockery of shit.
With visions from videos and porn mags
Turning thoughts to thongs and gags,
Will his loins and desires lewd,
Find comfort with their contents spewed?
Another victim, chose by fate,
Will see the sky!
But not the mark upon his slate.
No homage!
In his kingdom of lustful dream
Where the pink pointer reigns supreme.

CHILD PROSTITUTE
(CYNICISM'S BABY)

Good at school - nobody's fool
Protuberances, exuberances.
Always with watchful eye
What might fall from the sky.
Wants from life all that's best
Hates rejection - loathes the pest.
Watches those girls of the night
Portrayed by lamp and car headlights.
Junior school, but her dreams
Centred on men of means
They can be tall, short or small,
She really doesn't care at all.
Cast aside those schoolgirl socks
For high heeled shoes, skirts that shock.
Her ample cleavage on display
More they see - the more they pay
Knows the chat they like to hear
Suck them in and buy some gear.
Rogered by nobles, rogues and pimps
Gives her all and never skimps,
'Sees the skies' tells her lies
Touch the man - see him rise,
Fucks them all and doesn't care
Then goes home to her teddy bear.

Nursery Rhyme and Reason

Within the reach of all hands
Each child of innocence stands.

'Half a pound of tuppenny rice'
'Half a pound of treacle'

Good Lord keep, and protect them please,
From all accidents - and people!

'Pat-a-cake, Pat-a-cake bakers man'
'Bake us a cake faster than'

Sweet temptation that lurks each day,
Threatening to mar children's play.

'Jack and Jill'
'Went up the hill'

Those infant sons and daughters,
Mighty one, repel the troubled waters.

'Little Bo-Peep has lost her sheep'
'And knows not where to find them'

One above, safe guide them home,
Leave no sad tales behind them.

'Ring a ring o' roses'
'A pocket full of rye'

Meet their needs - Destroy the seeds,
Spare their tears with watchful eye.

SHADOW AT THE SCHOOL GATE

For each child, vulnerability is
Akin to the turn of a circle,
A hoop at play or, ring a ring o' roses.
Their destiny revolving like a chamber
Of spent cartridges firing pin set
By an unknown hand, awaiting a
Gentle squeeze by the finger of fate.

The hand in velvet glove that primes
The weapon of destruction snags not
On rough flesh, but is fashioned on
The softness that dwells in innocence.
Mentor to its demise, master of
The manipulative.

Somewhere he is there waiting, watching,
Dreaming, living the fantasy of
His sickness. A pied-piper nursery
Songs played, rehearsed and sweetly
Sung - Born of Depravity.

COME THE ZOMBIES

Beware! Human Puppet,
Animation's Toy.
What hand controls
Your strings?
Gives birth to
Daily song and dance,
Chords on which
Life's music is played.

Vulnerable marionette,
Cherish those moments.
For they who live
No melodies,
Will seek control of
Bodies that flap like
Broken wings,
And manipulate to
Dance in their Delight.

For they are made
Of no music.
Unborn in life's
Orchestration, and
Bear the silence
Of endless interlude.
Awaiting the drum of
A heart, that will pound
As theirs.

DEMISE OF A THESPIAN

Life long entertainer, now in demise.
No more with distinction to tread the boards.
His final performance staged
Attended only by his cast.
Laid unadorned, he will not perform.

This his swansong.
Cards shuffled reveal –
Spades sombre suit and
Destiny has played the trump card,
Earth moving, and grave the outcome.

His final appearance reviewed,
With a single word 'obituary'!
A cortège canopy of despair and
Myriad of floral bloom
Averts the eyes, but not
The sadness of his demise.

Slow, passes the motorcade of melancholy,
Forming alliance with
The dignity expected,
When surrendering the human form.
On earthly loan –
For an unknown period of time.

Mother Earth awaits
Not in firm grasp to hold
But with eternity's gentle touch
Holding endless vigil before
Total purloin of that
Not ours by divine right.

Earth and remembrance absorbs the texture
To minuscule finality and hearts
Beat strong in cherished memory.
'Farewell'
Theatrical weaver of dreams.

LEGLESS IN 1750

Bloweth more kind o' winter wind
What hast thou on thy mind?
Dost thou part clouds of snow
That on me, the moon shalt glow?
To bare my face, heart and soul.
Privy mine, as if 'twere thine?
Seek thee now my inner man
To meet some dire and devious plan?
Dost thy strength, that forests fell
Seek me for some earthly hell?
That thou shalt writ upon my grave
When serv'd my sentence as thy slave?
For I am but a righteous man
Though serve I not at God's hand,
A peasant of mere humble birth
And only to my peers hath worth.

Ne'er I do an evil deed
Perchance quaff my master's mead
And be'eth this such mortal sin
A new life, shalt I now begin.
To languish not in liquor's lust
Lest victim of thy mighty gust.
Banish thoughts of selfish glean
Live out my life in more serene,
Vanquish all sins of the heart
And from all sinners, stand apart.
Sup mead no more as dusk do fall
Make abstinence my wherewithal.
As I stumble now in drunken harm
To find my rest in Morpheus' arms
'Breathe thou light on a wretched man'.

REPENTANCE OF A CONDEMNED MAN

This last night, seen through bars,
The sky above awash with stars,
Drops of rain that never dry
Fall like God's tears from the sky.
- The stars show no pity.
Skies that watch, skies that see,
Care not to notice me.
Serve the sentence, bear the mark
With dignity to face the lark.
Can its sweet soft warble take
The venom from life's poison snake?

How that hair shirt chafes
Not intent flesh to find,
But within the confines of the mind.
No desire my human form
Precociously to adorn.
Those bars now weave a mental block
Gone the minute – gone the clock.
Each fleeting moment now, it seems,
Devoid of hope – devoid of dreams.

Cast, the die, left too late
That joyous trip to Heaven's gate.
A last foot now on Earth's firm sod
Lost the way – "Forgive me, God".

THE GRAVE ROBBER

Across the churchyard's sacred ground
And consecrated pall,
Fell the step of one intent
To reap a gruesome haul.
At dead of night and out of sight
He worked the darkness fall.

To seize the bodies buried there
He worked with frenzied force.
Toil and slave to rob the grave
With a strength to match the horse
As he tirelessly moved the holy earth
In this shameful intercourse.

And not once did it occur
As he worked and toiled there
That never would he take a step
To tread the heavenly stair
But dig a hole, that would leave his soul,
Floating on the air.

And as he laboured
No call of conscience came,
But to dig and desecrate the graves,
Those within to raise again.
Bodies, whose rest in peace
Would never be the same.

No show of pity or remorse
For this sin on human creed,
But driven by a deadly force
More potent than mere greed.
Accompanied by a tortured soul,
Where the devil had sown his seed.

The darkened sky hid from view
Stars and moon's thrown light.
As if to shield the evil deed
From heaven and celestial sight,
And around him ghostly spectres danced
In shrouds, with faces white.

The dance his eyes did not perceive,
Or of them be aware.
Their chant to fall upon deaf ears,
He had a cross to bear.
Unnoticed, fragrance from the yew
Did float upon night's air.

For in this very same church
He took the oath and vow,
At marriage rites in God's own sight
'My worldly goods endow'.
Destined to hide, from spouse's eyes
Grim cargoes handled now.

To be looked upon with dire disdain
Life's blessing - the obtuse,
Now for this wretched sinful man
Little, left to choose.
Success, to bring the guinea's gold,
To fail, the hangman's noose.

DUST TO DUST

Slowly turns the spool of life
Storing memories, camera to
Moments savoured then cast like
Old clothing, or a cloak spanning
Seas in which we paddle or drown.
Carrying our daily fortunes floating
Like leaves on the river of life.
Never to reach oceans of eternity.

Gather those leaves from the bough,
Freshen each stem feel the vibrance
Live in their radiance. For in the
Passing of our autumn they will capitulate
To winter's demise, crumble, trodden
Under foot. Returning to the earth
From which their seed of life –
Promised so much.

FORGOTTEN

Many years his life has spanned,
Denied now warmth of human hand.
To exist forgotten and alone
Quick, cut to the very bone.
Who cares now to review his fate?
In timeless void – Just sit and wait.

Muscle and sinew wasting away,
Felt the taint of human decay
Eyes that see, but not perceive
'The grim reaper' waiting at his sleeve.
No attempt to reserve his plot,
Captive of misfortune's squat.

No one will recall which day,
Stole his last lonely breath away.
Victim of the forty thieves,
His soul now floats on autumn leaves.
To settle in dust upon the ground
No trace of footprint to be found.

UNSEEN, HIDDEN IN JOURNEY AND SONG

Feathered of throat, the metal bird
To alight on welcoming airport,
Rio's Sugar Loaf reflected in blue sea.
Matched by the awe of its surroundings
Where pulsating ribboned beaches heave life.
Basking affluent tourists,
Self-appointed Princes, Playboys and Escapees
Sun-drenched, sweat drenched - tanning,
Held in spellbound infinity, mesmerised and content.
Formationed like ants awaiting their annual flight,
Lilos and beach chairs launching pads of indulgence
Workers, ply their trade dreaming of
Cruzeiro* laden satchels, pockets heavy with
Seasonal prosperity - however short lived.
Centre stage on Copacabana's golden mile the
Welcome of another 'Hotel California'
Equal to any fired by the imagination of
Eagle's swoop - such a lovely place!
From whose windows to view
'Pretty, Pretty Boys' of the beach,
In cavorting homage to their current Goddess
Of desire, wealth and wanton.
A motor bus passes, destination 'Ipanema'
Home of that special girl, beauty's myth
Glamourised by song (a recluse within its lyrics).
Where the sunset Motel nestles in infamous glory,
Terminus of buses, taxis and accompanied pleasure seekers.

Back at Copacabana the calm of Sabbath Sunday
Is broken by throngs of soccer bound devotees.
Bright striped attire allotted to their gladiatorial heroes
Fluminez. Champions whatever today's outcome at the
Maricana.
Impatiently they await victory, bringing further joy
Hope and reason to their existence.
Almost unseen, ignored, hills stretch
Favella laden well into the distance
Oozing poverty, disease, hunger. Resentment seething inert
Deep and oppressed. In an unsung Heaven or Hell
Where the Cruzeiro* in abundance is 'La Dolce Vita'
Its lack of Depravation, Despondency, Death.

* *Unit of Brazilian currency at this time.*

JOURNEY THROUGH SPAIN

Through Pamplona's deserted streets
In dark of night the amigo sleeps
Each Pablo, Paco seen by day
Now rest in somnolent array.

Angry bulls put to flight
Calm in silence of the night
Picadors, their arrows spent
In mutilation's dire contempt.

The wild sirocco blowing high
Seldom steadfast often sly.
Onward journey, new delights
Slowly passing Valencia's lights.

To unlit highways, late moonbeams.
Destination of our dreams,
As morning dawn meets the eyes
Now bathed in sun's early rise.

Warming, past Altea –
All the way through to Denia.

FLIGHT

Oh metal bird, that flies so high
Carry me away!
Clouds below like a carpet of snow,
The sky above pure cerulean.
All around a peaceful void.
To cruise with such ease and grace,
Near, yet so far from outer space.

Now to awaken from morning dreams
And savour the sight of sun's early beams.
That shine more bright with every ray,
Giving birth to another day.
Such a wondrous sight
As dawn throws its early light.

Then a gentle moment of joy
As clouds float by,
High up in the morning sky.
Oh metal bird, with comfort of wing,
If only you too could sing
And join me in a lullaby,
My trusty conveyor up high in the sky.

CASTLES IN THE AIR

He built a tree house
Deep in the forest of dreams.
A childhood retreat
Spanning the passing of time.
On earth below
Pounding footbeats reverberate
The many years seeking
An idyllic existence.
Where black is upon white,
Day follows night
In meticulous precision.
But branches move ceaselessly
Rendering the house insecure,
Future precarious - dependent on
Changing winds of fortune and fate.
Gale force, moderate, each day
Different. Slowly destroying the
Paper thin walls of
Castles in the air.

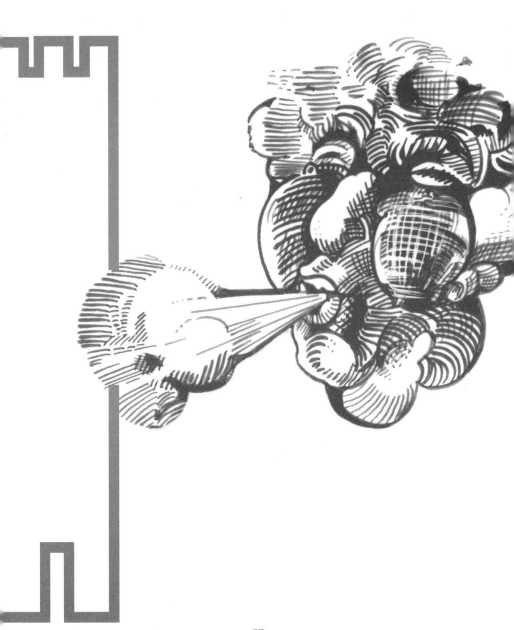

FLEDGLINGS

Across winter's stark terrain
Spreads the green tide. Spring buds
Burst their bonds of languidity
Sun shedding its winter overcoat.
Earth exhales in the season's
New-found glory.
A glory shared with new arrivals
Nature's Animation borne on wings
Of wonder, facing now the mystery
And challenge of life.
Fledglings, young wings not yet
Mobilised, free fall from their
Nests in precarious descent like
Shuttlecocks or on invisible parachutes.
Stumbling dazed into their
New world.

CARING

The gift of speech
Is within the reach
Of most to learn
And some to teach.

The art of love
Sent from on high,
Will sometimes visit
Or pass us by.

But in most of us
That's sadly missing,
Is the time to care
And desire to listen.

YOU SHOULDN'T HAVE TOLD ME MUM

I am the onion man
Who cried at the bank,
I am the Sinatra
Who could never be Frank,
I am the Tripod
That walks with a limp,
I am the child
Spawned by a wimp.

I am the Mentor
Of sorrow and pain,
I am the alien
Who made it to Spain,
I am the singer
Who can't sing a note,
I am the victim
Knife at his throat.

I am the egg
That fell from the wall,
I am the dwarf
Who never stood tall
I am the loner
Who feels the pain,
I am the sunbather
Caught by the rain.

I am the offspring
Held by the mouse,
I am the black sheep
At Somerset House,
I am the error
Trapped here on earth,
I am the Bastard
An outcast at birth.

I am.

MENTOR

Remember, I am the voice
You plucked from the womb,
Drawing tight the umbilical cord.
Soothing my cries of desperation, the
Search for recognition - gifted only
To kings, princes, The chosen few.

Your mentor's cloak covering
My dreams, your dreams the
Recognition we seek.
Aspirations, yours in retrospect
Mine yet awaiting birth,
May we wreak no abortion.

THE COMING OF AGE

It was not her beauty
Caught my eye and my breath
But her radiance, softly hidden
Like the sun with dusk closing.
The piquant purity that
Brimmed naïve, impinging on
Heart and soul.

I have often trod paths of liaison
Plumbed the depths of deceit
Tendering the rose of many thorns.
But this was different, somehow
Likened to love, the word abused
By philanderers and charlatans
Use in abuse.

Forget the firm flesh, carnal
Delights, exploitation, for those
Young arms bore welcome.
Paradoxically age and youth
Blending, self-reproach melting
Like snow in the new warmth of
A summer sun.

TOUCHING UTOPIA

Fingers reach out
Nerve ends caressed by expectation.
The mind, like a harpist
Searches for a note.
Awaiting, sweet the chord
Not only struck when music flows.

A touch, those fingers expressive and tender,
Pale sensuous, pink tipped promises of ecstasy.
Now to dream and wish,
For more than just digital fusion,
Progression to pleasures untapped.
No vocal discourse, eyes meet
Then return to pressing palms,
Each gentle touch speaking a thousand words.

'If music be the food of love'
Stay the symphony,
Till the score has been savoured.
Ingested, digested, to feed
The need of fulfilment.
Not a singular selfish experience
But a shared and beautiful liaison
Of body and soul.

Blood flows under sensitive skin fusing.
A longing for more.
Each movement and touch teasingly
Telegraphs a message of inner desire.
What lies beneath? Words would intrude
On this interlude of touch and feel.
Fingers winging a message of intent,
'Open those gates', that I may enter
The inner sanctum.

Too Busy

"I don't have the time!"
Say it often and it will rhyme.
Too busy to do things - just say
"Best left for another day".
I sit and wait, twiddle my thumbs,
But tomorrow never comes.

I often fret I'm always so busy
The thought of which makes me feel quite dizzy.
To do all those things that others do
Would be so fine - if only I had the time.
I must concede, let's make it clear,
Someone had the time, or I'd not be here.

I see all those people hurrying past,
Doing things oh so fast.
All those moments every day,
But how soon can they pass away?
How do I cope? It amazes me!
I must sit and think - now let me see.

My mentor is solid as a rock,
To me, a friend, to all others 'Mister Clock';
I find him unique and quite sublime –
He always seems to have the time!
Not to watch him would ruin my day,
As then I would have no time for play.

It would be lovely to sit at home all day,
But "I don't have the time"
So I wrote this poem instead.
It would be nice to have ended it
With a rhyme – "I didn't have time",
But I made the time!

MY SPECIAL ONE

My special one
You wield the knife
That no incision
Would match the pain
Of your derision.
Those moments from another day
Did heavy on conscience prey,
But lift us to a higher plane
And risk in life - although insane.

A time when
Infatuation, mindless greed
And our vanity,
More than matched
Mere sanity.
Emotions vent, with no tears
To mask the tomorrow of our fears.
Lips untouched, avoided embrace
Shielding us from worldly disgrace.

Then to linger
In a timeless void,
Forged in love's embryo
That convention of life
Destroyed.
And though fate did not for us sing,
Until death, shall I wear your ring
Remembering that message - from the eye
Which no one knows - but you and I.

INDEX OF FIRST LINES